CW01512898

Original title:

Fallow Metals Inside the Wizard Yarn

Author: Olivia Oja

ISBN HARDBACK: 978-1-80563-066-1

ISBN PAPERBACK: 978-1-80564-587-0

Threads of Fate and Wandering Wishes

In shadows deep where whispers weave,
The fae have spun their tales to leave.
A tapestry of dreams untold,
In silver threads and bits of gold.

The moonlight dances on the ground,
Where ancient secrets can be found.
Each step we take, a fateful choice,
In every heart, a hidden voice.

The stars above, like lanterns bright,
Guide weary souls through endless night.
A flicker here, a spark of chance,
In twilight's glow, we find our dance.

Through winding paths of tangled fate,
We chase the dreams that come too late.
Yet hope remains, a steadfast flame,
That every heart knows well by name.

So let us weave our wishes bold,
With strands of love and tales of old.
For in our hands, the threads unite,
And weave a world alive with light.

Secrets Woven in Stardust

In twilight's grip, the stars align,
Whispers speak of tales divine.
A moonlit path, where shadows play,
Secrets kept till break of day.

With every twinkle, dreams take flight,
In the silence of the night.
Mysterious glimmers guide our way,
Through realms where ancient shadows sway.

A tapestry of light unfurls,
Each thread a story, softly swirls.
The sky, an open book above,
In starlit ink, we find our love.

With hearts ablaze, we spin our fates,
In this dance, the cosmos waits.
For secrets whispered by the stars,
Reveal our hopes, our hidden scars.

So, let us chase the drifting glow,
Through cosmic pathways we shall flow.
In every shimmer, magic blooms,
In woven dreams where stardust looms.

Lurking Echoes of Forged Magic

In shadows deep, the echoes call,
Of ancient spells and hidden thrall.
Through corridors of time we roam,
In search of magic, we call home.

With every step, the whispers grow,
As secrets twine in ebb and flow.
The air electrifies with might,
A spark ignites the edge of night.

Beneath the veil of moonlit dreams,
Reality bends at magic's seams.
We dance among the flames of fate,
Where echoes linger, small and great.

A tale of bravery, bold and vast,
Where shadows flit and moments pass.
In every heart, a flicker glows,
Of forged magic in their throes.

So, tread with caution, brave of heart,
For magic's wild, a fearsome art.
In lurking echoes, truth shall bloom,
Unravel mysteries in the gloom.

The Tapestry of Forgotten Sorcery

In twilight's glow, the stories weave,
Of sorcery, some can't believe.
Threads of gold and shadows dark,
In every strand, a whispered spark.

Forgotten spells in twilight hide,
As magic flows like a gentle tide.
We search for truths in tapestry,
Where past and present dance so free.

Each thread a memory, tightly spun,
Of battles fought and victories won.
In every knot, a fate entwined,
With echoes of what once aligned.

So brave the heart, ignite the flame,
In this vast realm, seek out the name.
Sorcery's touch, though long since dried,
Still flickers bright, no need to hide.

The tapestry unfolds its art,
In colors vibrant, here we start.
With wonder rising, let us see,
The hidden magic, wild and free.

Veils of Elemental Whimsy

In nature's dance, the elements play,
With water's grace and fire's sway.
Wind whispers tales of ancient lore,
While earth beholds what came before.

Beneath the moon's soft silver glow,
A world of wonders starts to flow.
With every ripple, dreams take flight,
As whimsy sparkles in the night.

In stormy skies, the thunder calls,
While grace of rain in silence falls.
Each drop a promise, strong and bold,
Of stories yet to be retold.

Embrace the stir of nature's tune,
As elements dance beneath the moon.
In every breeze, there lies a spark,
Of whimsical tales in shadows dark.

So let us bask in nature's might,
As earth and sky unite in flight.
In veils of magic, we shall find,
The whimsy living, intertwined.

Gilded Dreams on Ether Winds

In twilight glow, the stars align,
Whispers weave through threads divine.
With every breath, the magic swells,
In hushed tones, the ether tells.

A tapestry of dreams unfolds,
In jests of fate, the heart beholds.
With gossamer strands, our spirits dance,
In the gilded light, we find our chance.

On silken paths where shadows play,
Wonders awaken with each new day.
The winds of change, with gentle song,
Guide the lost souls to where they belong.

With every spark, a tale takes flight,
Carried aloft on wings of night.
In realms unseen, where wishes bloom,
Our hearts ignite, dispelling gloom.

In dreams of gold, we find our peace,
The ether's whispers never cease.
In this enchanted, wondrous scheme,
We sail the seas of gilded dreams.

The Alchemist's Hidden Weft

In shadows deep, the secrets lie,
An alchemist's weave beneath the sky.
With whispered spells and cunning art,
He transforms the world, a daring start.

The potion's glow, a fleeting sight,
In still of night, it spirals bright.
With precision pure, each element,
Becomes a force, a wise ascent.

Through flasks and vials, his visions flow,
Gold from lead, a fable's glow.
The hidden weft, so deftly spun,
In every heart, the spark begun.

The sacred truth, it flickers low,
In every choice, the seeds we sow.
With alchemical grace, we take our stand,
Crafting wonders with a steady hand.

In the quiet dusk where dreams converge,
The alchemist's heart begins to surge.
Each drop infused with ancient lore,
Unlocks the paths forevermore.

Shimmering Twists of Fate

In twilight's grasp, the tales unfold,
Shimmering tales of the brave and bold.
With every turn, our choices gleam,
We dance upon the edge of a dream.

The cosmic hand reshapes our plight,
Beneath the veil of starlit night.
Twists of fate weave through the air,
In every moment, magic's flare.

With bated breath, we chase the light,
In shimmering threads, our futures write.
With laughter's chime and tears that flow,
We face the paths that we don't know.

Destinies beckon, both near and far,
In the dance of time, we are the star.
Each winding road, a treasure gained,
In golden hues, our joy retained.

Embrace the twists, each rise and fall,
For in the journey, we hear the call.
In shimmering light, our hearts connect,
As fate's sweet kiss leaves us in awe.

Fabric of the Arcane Realm

In shadows where the whispers weave,
A fabric spun from dreams we cleave.
Threads of magic, rich and bold,
In the arcane realm, our tales unfold.

With every stitch, the story grows,
In hidden corners, ancient flows.
Embroidered truths in vibrant hues,
Awaken wonder, and hope renews.

Through realms of thought, our spirits soar,
Each tapestry holds an open door.
With every breath, the looms align,
In echoes deep, the fates entwine.

The arcane's heart, a pulsing beat,
In swirling mists, we find our seat.
With magic's thread, we boldly weave,
In realms unseen, our hearts believe.

As moonlight bathes the sacred ground,
New stories rise, enchantment found.
In each soft fold, a journey's call,
We stand united, and never fall.

Chronicles of the Arcane Loom

In twilight's hush, the shadows weave,
Silent threads of tales believe.
With every twist, a secret spun,
Fables dance till night is done.

From ancient hands, the patterns grow,
Emerald sights in twilight's glow.
Echoes whisper of realms untold,
In the fabric, legends fold.

A loom that knows of stars and moons,
Each strand a hymn, each beam a tune.
Gather the dreams from realms afar,
Weaving wishes where wishes are.

Through threads of time, the weaver glides,
Beneath the sky where twilight hides.
Mysteries tangled in silvered lace,
Awaken the magic of endless space.

Once spun the tales, forever free,
In the loom's embrace, they come to be.
A chronicle born from dusk to dawn,
Arcane whispers in silence drawn.

The Hidden Forge of Fantasia

In shadows deep, the forge aglow,
Crafting dreams we yearn to know.
Hammers dance on brightened steel,
Where the pulse of magic is real.

With fiery breath, the ancients craft,
In the twilight, hear their laughter waft.
Each chosen spark, a flicker's fate,
Forging wonders, we wait, we wait.

The hidden realm where wishes cling,
Beneath the wings of ethereal spring.
Sparks that shimmer in moonlit night,
Illustrate tales in colors bright.

Time is bent in a crafty dance,
A shapesmith's play, a fateful chance.
From molten dreams, new worlds arise,
In the forge of stars, behold the skies.

Each sword and shield, a tale forged true,
In Fantasia's heart, dreams come into view.
Whispers of legends in every beat,
As magic and might together meet.

Woven Whispers of the Ancients

In the stillness where echoes dwell,
Whispers rise like a distant bell.
Songs of ancients in threads entwined,
Lost in the folds of space and time.

With every breath, a story's kiss,
Woven whispers weave worlds of bliss.
Cloaks of wisdom, wrapped in light,
Glimmers of truth, a filtered sight.

The loom of ages hums a tune,
Dancing in shadows, beneath the moon.
Softly they call, the spirits near,
In tapestry bold, their tales appear.

In every fiber, the past resides,
Threads of glory, where time abides.
Ancient hands, with skillful art,
Ignite the magic in every heart.

The whispers guide to realms unspun,
Where destinies twist like silken run.
A woven path, the ancients share,
In every thread, their truth laid bare.

Spectres of Transmuted Threads

In shifting shadows, spectres glide,
Transmuted threads their secrets hide.
Flickering forms of light and dark,
They dart through realms, leave not a mark.

From silver strands to shadows deep,
In twilight's grasp, their stories seep.
A tapestry of fate untold,
In every ghostly fold, behold.

Beneath the veil where dreams entwine,
Spectres seek what once was mine.
They whisper soft in ancient tongues,
Tales of glory their heartstrings strung.

With every breath, a story swells,
In transmuted echoes, time compels.
A thread of fate, a spectral guide,
Weaving destinies, side by side.

Through veils of night, the loom does hum,
In mystic dances, they become.
The spectres weave what lies ahead,
In threads of magic, where none have tread.

The Rough Beauty of Hidden Gems

In caverns deep, where light forgets,
The whispered tales of old regrets.
Each stone a story yet untold,
A shimmering truth, in shadows bold.

Beneath the soil, the secrets sigh,
In quiet realms where lost dreams lie.
Emeralds glint with emerald grace,
As nature's hand shapes time and space.

With dust and grit, they find their way,
In rugged forms where wild hearts play.
The gem within, a soul unbound,
In roughened edges, beauty found.

For every crack, a path to light,
In darkness blooms a heart's delight.
These hidden treasures sing so sweet,
In every pulse, the world's heartbeat.

Awake, arise, the world awaits,
With courage wrapped in fate's own gait.
Embrace the gems that life bestows,
In roughened beauty, gardens grow.

Shadows of Enigma in the Weaving

Beneath the moonlit, silver thread,
In ancient woods where whispers spread,
The shadows dance in mystic lore,
Holding secrets forevermore.

With every stitch, a tale is spun,
In tangled webs where shadows run.
The figures sway, both fierce and kind,
In fabric dreams, the heart entwined.

Through twilight's haze, the shapes emerge,
Pulsing softly like a gentle surge.
They beckon forth the brave and bold,
In threads of silver, stories unfold.

What lies within the woven night?
In borrowed grace, the heart takes flight.
The enigma calls, we draw so near,
To whispers' song that only dreams hear.

A tapestry of light and shade,
In woven realms, the truth is laid.
In shadows' clutch, the magic stirs,
With every weave, the world concurs.

Spools of Myth and Magic

In corners dim, where whispers twine,
The old spools sit, their tales divine.
With threads of gold and midnight blue,
They weave the fables known to few.

Each pull reveals a world anew,
From ancient lands where legends grew.
With every stitch, a magic cast,
In timeless myths, from first to last.

A dance of dragons, knights in flight,
The shimmer of stars on endless night.
In tangled yarns, their hearts reside,
Through every tale, the realms collide.

With each spool spun, the past awakes,
The echoes of time as history breaks.
In colors bright, the stories gleam,
In woven dreams, we find our theme.

So take a thread, make stories flow,
In spools of magic, let your heart glow.
For in each twist, a spark ignites,
Illuminating the darkest nights.

The Golden Silhouette of Dreams

When dusk descends, the sky aglow,
A silhouette of dreams we know.
In shadows long and whispers light,
We chase the stars, igniting night.

With every breath, the hopes arise,
In golden sparks that kiss the skies.
The journey leads through realms unseen,
Where wishes bloom in shades of green.

With quiet hearts and open hands,
We walk the paths of ancient lands.
In fleeting moments, magic brews,
In every touch, the world renews.

The golden threads of fate entwine,
We find our way, our hearts align.
In every heartbeat, dreams take form,
And from the dusk, a light is born.

So chase the silhouette, the gleam,
In every waking note, a dream.
For life is but a fleeting glance,
In golden hues, we find our dance.

Glints of Brilliance in Twisted Iron

In shadows deep, where echoes play,
Twisted iron holds its sway.
A silent forge, a whispered cry,
Beneath the stars, the embers lie.

Glistening sparks in midnight's breath,
Crafting hope amidst the death.
Glints of promise, fierce and bright,
Dance with shadows through the night.

Each hammer's strike a tale to tell,
Of dreams entwined, of heaven and hell.
An anvil sings a haunting tune,
Of daring hearts and silver moons.

Around the fire, legends weave,
Of iron forged and webs we leave.
A tapestry of fate and fear,
In every shard, a glimmer near.

So raise your voice, let secrets flow,
In twisted iron, let brilliance grow.
For every spark that lights the way,
Hints at tomorrow's bright array.

A Yarn of Myths and Wonders

In a realm where shadows dwell,
Myths are spun like fragrant spell.
Threaded through with whispers light,
A dance of stories, day and night.

From ancient woods, the tales arise,
Beneath the watchful, starry skies.
A tapestry of brave and bold,
Each stitch a memory retold.

Wonders bloom in courage's name,
Fires ignite with wild acclaim.
In hidden glades, the faeries sing,
Their laughter bright, a gentle ring.

Legends flow like rivers wide,
Carving paths where dreams abide.
In every clock, a story waits,
Unfolding softly as fate dictates.

So gather 'round, let voices soar,
For myths and wonders, evermore.
Embrace the lore and set it free,
A yarn entwined in mystery.

The Tapestry of Forgotten Dreams

Woven threads of silver and gold,
In quiet corners, stories told.
Each dream a stitch, each wish a thread,
In shadows cast where memories tread.

Echoes linger in twilight's glow,
Of hopes once high, now lost below.
But in the weave, there lies a spark,
A light to guide us from the dark.

Tangled paths of laughter and tears,
We thread our hearts through fleeting years.
In every fiber, joys and fears,
Crafting visions that reappear.

Forgotten dreams whisper at night,
Awakening visions, taking flight.
In every knot, a lesson learned,
In every loop, a passion burned.

So cherish the threads that time will hold,
In the tapestry, let legends unfold.
For in the fabric of who we are,
Lies the path to our own bright star.

Simmering Secrets Across the Spokes

In silence deep, the wheels do turn,
Secrets simmer, twists and churn.
Across the spokes, their stories wind,
A chorus of the hush, unkind.

Beneath the surface, whispers low,
Of journeys taken, tales to sow.
In shadows cast, the truth does creep,
While dreams are woven, softly steep.

A flicker here, a spark appears,
In every sigh, the weight of years.
Glimmers flash through crooked lanes,
As time unveils its hidden veins.

With every spin, a lesson learned,
As dreams collide and passions burned.
Secrets simmer, quietly stir,
Across the spokes, where shadows blur.

So heed the tales that distance shows,
In every path that silence knows.
For within the spokes of life's dear ride,
Lies the magic we cannot hide.

Celestial Tapestries of Lost Ages

In skies adorned with threads of gold,
Ancient stories of the stars unfold.
Wisps of dreams, like feathers light,
Whisper secrets of the night.

Each constellation weaves a fate,
Entwined in time, we contemplate.
Moments linger, lost yet near,
Echoes held in stardust dear.

Through ages past, the stories flow,
Guided by a celestial glow.
In every twinkle, shadows play,
Marking paths of yesterday.

The moon looks down with silver grace,
Upon the tales that time must trace.
Each radiant burst, a voice from beyond,
In the cosmic dance, we are drawn.

So let us weave with threads of dreams,
A tapestry made of moonlit beams.
For in this web of light and dark,
We find our place, a timeless spark.

The Weight of History in Silver Strings

Threads of memory, tightly spun,
Echoes linger when day is done.
History hums a whispered tune,
Carried softly beneath the moon.

With every note, a tale takes flight,
Woven into the fabric of night.
Silver strings pulled taut with care,
Binding moments lost in air.

A touch of sorrow, a dash of grace,
In the shadows where dreams embrace.
In quiet corners where time suspends,
The past and present, resilient friends.

As lanterns flicker, memories bloom,
Illuminating the silence of gloom.
Each heartbeat a story, rich and vast,
Connecting futures with echoes of past.

So, let us listen, let us learn,
From silver strings, the ancient yarn.
For in the weight of what has been,
We find the strength to begin again.

Midst the Twilight, Secrets Unraveled

As dusk descends, the day concedes,
Whispers flourish among the reeds.
In twilight's grasp, shadows entwined,
Secrets linger, waiting to find.

The air is thick with ancient lore,
Of battles fought on a distant shore.
With every breeze, a tale is spun,
Unraveling dreams 'til the night has begun.

Stars peek out, their eyes aglow,
Bearing witness to all we know.
Mysteries dance in the fading light,
Revealing truths hidden from sight.

In every heartbeat, stories rise,
A tapestry woven beneath the skies.
So gather 'round as the shadows blend,
For in this dusk, beginnings extend.

The world holds secrets, profound and deep,
Waiting silently, wishing to seep.
Through twilight's door, they softly creep,
Unraveled gently, while we sleep.

Transmuted Echoes in Starlit Realms

Among the stars, where echoes gleam,
Whispers carry on a cosmic dream.
Transmuted tales on astral winds,
Floating softly where time rescinds.

Every flicker, a story's breath,
Gliding through the veils of death.
In every twinkle, ancient light,
An echo lingers, fierce and bright.

Dance of shadows, weave of fate,
In starlit realms where moments sate.
The universe hums a vibrant song,
Calling us forth, where we belong.

Time dissolves in the vast embrace,
Of infinite wonder, a boundless space.
Here we transform, in radiant hue,
Echoes of old, reborn anew.

So let us wander, heartbeats aligned,
In the starlit realms, where we find,
That every echo, every gleam,
Is part of a grander cosmic dream.

In the Heart of Enchanted Looms

In the heart where secrets blend,
Threads of magic spin and bend,
Whispers dance in twilight's glow,
Where the ancient stories flow.

In the shadows, dreams take flight,
Starlit patterns paint the night,
Fingers trace a woven fate,
Each stitch holds a world innate.

Tales of old wrapped tight in twine,
Hold your breath, let fate align,
For in this web lies more than lore,
A spell to crack the endless door.

Echoes weave in tender grace,
Crimson threads, a warm embrace,
Surrounding hearts with magic's thread,
Unraveling all that could be read.

So linger here where titans roam,
In this place, you find your home,
With every twist, a chance to glean,
The wonders lost and yet unseen.

Tangles of Memory in Silvered Dust

Amidst the shelves of silvered dust,
Whispers of time in silence rust,
Each grain a tale, a fleeting sigh,
Echoes of laughter, dreams that fly.

Hands of fate entwine the past,
Tangled moments, shadows cast,
In hushed corners, bright embers glint,
Stories linger, no air, no hint.

Fleeting visions take their place,
In the mind's eye, a tender trace,
Memory dances, a waltz so sweet,
Laced with laughter, both bitter and neat.

Through the veil where echoes dwell,
History weaves its subtle spell,
In silver dust, a universe spins,
From the losses, every win begins.

So let the past within you soar,
In the tangle, find the lore,
With every breath, the echoes hum,
In the silence, stories come.

The Muffled Beats of Time's Loom

In chambers deep where shadows lie,
The loom of time weaves low and high,
Each heartbeat whispers faint and clear,
An endless rhythm, far yet near.

Threads of moments, soft and frail,
Tales of triumph, tales of wail,
Every tick marks hopes and fears,
In the silence, catch your tears.

A pattern shifts in twilight's breath,
The dance of life, a waltz with death,
As memories fade, others bloom,
In the dark, we seal our doom.

Yet in the weave, a spark remains,
Through all the joy and all the pains,
With every pattern, life's embrace,
Find the beauty, find your place.

So listen close, let heartstrings twine,
For in this beat, our souls entwine,
Time's muffled song, an ancient lore,
In every loop, we live once more.

Orbs of Light and Reflective Tones

Through the forest, lanterns glow,
Orbs of light, a gentle flow,
Reflective tones in shadows cast,
Echoes of present, whispers of past.

Hues of amber, soft and bright,
A symphony of day and night,
Floating softly, dreams take flight,
In the dance of the silver light.

Each orb a tale, a moment's grace,
Lost in time, a warm embrace,
In reflective pools, we see our soul,
Merging shadows, making whole.

As twilight fades, they start to wane,
Yet in our hearts, they still remain,
A chorus bold in silence speaks,
In every heart, a truth that seeks.

So wander forth where glowworms weave,
Chase the shadows, dare believe,
For in the light, a world anew,
Orbs of wonder, waiting for you.

Mystical Fibers in Twilight

In twilight's weave, the magic spins,
With strands of light where shadows begin.
Secrets murmured in the air,
Whispers twinkle, beyond compare.

The colors dance, a vibrant glow,
Each thread a story, waiting to show.
The moonlight drapes a silver shawl,
Enveloping dreams that softly call.

Among the trees, the fibers sway,
Guiding the lost who've lost their way.
A tapestry of whispered fears,
Woven deeply through the years.

Beneath the stars, where wishes rise,
A loom of fate, where magic lies.
Weaving hope in every thread,
A world where only dreams are bred.

So let the twilight take its flight,
Embrace the magic, hold it tight.
For in the fibers, secrets gleam,
In the twilight's fabric, a hidden dream.

Threads of Silvered Secrets

In the stillness of the night,
Threads of silver shine so bright.
Whispers born from ancient lore,
Secrets lingering at the core.

With every stitch, a tale unfolds,
Through the silence, the mystery holds.
Each fiber sings a timeless song,
Echoes of where the heart belongs.

The shimmering weave of fate's design,
In every twist, the stars align.
Beneath the gaze of watchful skies,
The hidden truth never lies.

In shadows deep, the secrets play,
Tendrils drawn in a dance of sway.
A harmony of night's embrace,
As souls entwine in mystic lace.

So unravel the threads, set them free,
Let silver secrets be the key.
For in the heart of every thread,
Awaits the magic of what's been said.

The Loom of Enchantment

In the loom where dreams reside,
Enchantment flows, a gentle tide.
Each stitch a wish, each knot a prayer,
Woven with love and tender care.

Fingers dance on the delicate strings,
Crafting the magic that the heart brings.
The threads of fate, a vibrant swirl,
Spinning stories in a mystic whirl.

Amidst the shadows, a light will break,
Guiding the souls who dare to wake.
Through every weave, a path is drawn,
In the loom of enchantment, hope is born.

The tapestry whispers secrets old,
Of journeys lived and tales retold.
In the weft and warp, the magic glows,
Illuminating where the heart knows.

So sit a while, let the magic thread,
Wrap around the dreams in your head.
For in the loom of ageless night,
Every weave transforms into light.

Shadows of Arcane Filaments

In shadows deep, where secrets sigh,
Arcane filaments weave and fly.
With silken threads of whispered lore,
They bind the past forevermore.

Each filament, a tale untold,
In darkness, their mysteries unfold.
Veils of night embrace the light,
In shadow's dance, what is hidden is bright.

The fibers pulse with ancient power,
Echoing softly in twilight's hour.
In every twist, a magic spark,
Guiding the wanderers from the dark.

Among the trees, the filaments sing,
Luring the brave to seek the spring.
For in their depths lie stories bold,
Of adventures waiting to be told.

So tread with care, where shadows lean,
And let the threads of fate be seen.
For in the web of the arcane night,
Lies the promise of endless light.

Secrets of the Spinning Wheel

In shadows twirls the ancient thread,
Whispers of magic softly spread.
Each rotation, a secret to unfold,
Stories of eons, in fibers told.

The spindle hums a quiet tune,
Beneath the watchful gaze of moon.
In twilight's grasp, the secrets sigh,
Threads of fate that never die.

Glimmers dance on the spooled line,
Concealed truths, both yours and mine.
With every twist, a wish is spun,
A tapestry where dreams are won.

Cloaked in wonder, spun with care,
The weaver's heart laid truly bare.
With nimble hands, the story grows,
Of love and loss that time bestows.

So listen close; the wheel may weave,
A tale of hope that we believe.
In silken strands, our fate entwined,
Secrets of the heart, lovingly lined.

The Velvet Embrace of Worn Edges

In corners dark, the velvety weave,
Silk and dust in layers conceive.
A fabric whispers, soft yet grand,
The touch of memory, close at hand.

Worn edges speak of journeys past,
Of fleeting moments, shadows cast.
With every fold, the echo sings,
Of heartbeats close and gentle things.

Though frayed and torn, it holds so tight,
The velvet depths conceal the light.
In twilight's hush, the stories stay,
Of laughter shared and dreams at play.

Embracing warmth in tender seams,
The fabric carries all our dreams.
A quilt of life, stitched with grace,
In worn edges, we find our place.

So let the velvet wrap us near,
A timeless bond that draws us here.
In memories sewn, we softly weave,
A tapestry of love to believe.

Riddles of the Hushed Loom

The hush of night, where secrets loom,
Fingers dance in twilight's gloom.
A silent riddle in the threads,
Where every stitch in silence treads.

Woven whispers, soft and low,
Tales of wonders we long to know.
With nimble grace, the yarns entwine,
In shadows deep, the dreams align.

Each pass and pull a story bent,
A canvas rich with time well spent.
The loom entwines both joy and grief,
An ancient craft, a heart's belief.

So can you hear the silent call,
Of riddles etched in fabric's thrall?
With each creation, so profound,
The hush of weaving, magic found.

In twilight's grasp, let spirits weave,
The secrets all that we believe.
For in the loom, the truth shall bloom,
A tapestry of destiny's room.

A Tangle of Enchanted Twine

In the garden where shadows play,
A tangle of twine leads the way.
Around the trees and tangled vines,
Where softest whispers weave in lines.

The sun breaks through with golden rays,
A laughter caught in sunshine's gaze.
Each strand a story, tightly wound,
In every twist, a magic found.

Pull gently now, let secrets show,
The tangled paths where dreams can flow.
Through the leaves, the echoes sing,
Of all the hope that nature brings.

So wander deep, embrace the chance,
In the mesmerizing, twirling dance.
For in the fabric of this site,
The enchanted twine glows soft and bright.

With every knot, a bond is made,
In timeless play, we won't be swayed.
For love and laughter, intertwined,
A tangle of joy, forever twined.

The Magic Hidden in Dusty Crates

In a corner, hidden away,
Old crates gather shadows today.
A whisper of magic, soft and clear,
Promises of wonders, yet to appear.

Dust clings like memories, strong and tight,
Each creak and each rustle sparks delight.
A wand, a trinket, secrets untold,
Glories of past, just waiting to unfold.

The elder wood smells of stories grand,
With each gentle touch, dreams slip through hand.
Curiosities awake, bursting forth bright,
In the silence, the magic takes flight.

For hidden within the forgotten craft,
Are tales of joy, and mischief, and laughter.
Unlock these treasures with heartful debate,
And weave the enchantments, before it's too late.

As the dust swirls softly in soft candle glow,
A journey begins where no one can go.
In these dusty crates, lies a world quite vast,
Where the breath of the past whispers spells that will last.

Splinters of Light in the Old Tapestry

In the hall where shadows dance,
A tapestry shimmers, taking a chance.
Threads of gold weave stories of yore,
Splinters of light, forever explore.

With each thread pulled, a tale unfolds,
Mysteries hidden in stories retold.
Dancers in fabric, both fierce and bold,
Whispering secrets that never grow old.

The weaver's hand, a flickering spark,
Brought warmth to the night, dispersing the dark.
Patterns entwined, as fate's fingers play,
Crafting the dreams that lead hearts astray.

Each splinter of light, a moment caught,
In the weave of the universe, lessons are taught.
Woven connections, they shimmer and sing,
A symphony crafted with each tiny string.

So gaze at the tapestry, lost in time's snare,
Threads intertwining, casting a dare.
To seek out the light, and the stories they share,
In the tapestry's embrace, you'll find magic rare.

Requiem of Lost Luminaries

In the night sky, stars flicker and fade,
Whispers of light, in silence they wade.
Once they would shine, so vividly bright,
Now they are echoes, swallowed by night.

Each luminary carries a tale,
Of dreams that once bloomed, now frail.
In stillness they linger, a soft, gentle sigh,
A requiem sung for the sparks in the sky.

Past voices echo in shimmering mist,
Reminders of moments that would not be missed.
A dance of the cosmos, now marred by the dark,
Yet in memory's glow, still leaps a warm spark.

As twilight descends with a melancholic grace,
We gather the stories, each luminous trace.
For in every loss, there lingers a light,
A shared understanding that shines through the night.

And though stars may fade, their stories remain,
In all of our hearts, they dance in the rain.
With reverence we hold them, our lost luminaries,
In the silence of darkness, their legacy varies.

The Enigmatic Weave of the Universe

In the fabric of night, a pattern resides,
Woven with wonders, the cosmos confides.
Stitch by stitch, the mysteries form,
An enigmatic weave, radiant and warm.

Galaxies spiral, a delicate thread,
Colors collide where only dreams tread.
Black holes whisper secrets so deep,
In the cosmic embrace, all wonders sleep.

Time bends and reforms, a circle so vast,
Echoing moments, both future and past.
The universe dances, a ball of delight,
In its enigmatic weave, logic takes flight.

Weaving our tales through each celestial gate,
In the harmony of all, there's room for fate.
With stardust and echoes, our journeys align,
In this vast tapestry, our stories entwine.

So gaze at the night, find your place in the scheme,
Charted in starlight, the paths of a dream.
In the weave of the universe, forever we flow,
As mysteries unravel, new worlds we bestow.

The Alchemist's Secret Tapestry

In chambers deep where shadows play,
The alchemist weaves night and day.
With whispered words and potions bright,
He hunts for wisdom, longing for light.

Threads of truth, entwined with desire,
Mingle with dreams that never tire.
Mysteries cloaked in shades of gold,
In every stitch, a story unfolds.

The elements dance in laughter and glee,
As he captures the essence of mystery.
In every drop of enchanted brew,
Lies a world waiting, vast and new.

With a flick of his wrist, the tapestry sways,
Revealing secrets of long-lost days.
An alchemist's heart, forever inspired,
By visions of magic, endlessly wired.

So here in the dark, with whispers profound,
The threads of his craft circle around.
A tale of alchemy, twilight's embrace,
In every filament, time finds its place.

Threads of Time in Twilight's Grip

In twilight's hush, the clock strikes three,
Threads of time whisper, wild and free.
Each moment captured, shimmering bright,
Embroidered softly in the heart of night.

Memories linger, like shadows cast,
Woven together, futures and pasts.
A silver needle, stitching dreams true,
In the fabric of cosmos, old and new.

Every heartbeat, a thread pulled tight,
Binding the dark with threads of light.
As stars awaken in cosmic sighs,
Time dances gently beneath starlit skies.

An ancient loom hums its tune,
Crafting destinies under the moon.
While daylight wanes and shadows creep,
The stories of mortals in silence seep.

Each thread a whisper, a tale to unfold,
Of bravery, love, of legends bold.
In twilight's embrace, we find our place,
As time weaves its tapestry with grace.

A Dance of Lead and Gold

In markets bustling, amidst the throng,
Where laughter mingles with notes of song.
Gold glimmers brightly, a sight to behold,
While lead lies heavy, a burden untold.

A dance begins with the flick of a wrist,
As hope and despair in shadows twist.
With every step, a story is spun,
Of sweet victories and battles won.

The alchemist balances fate's cruel jest,
With lead's dark weight, he must invest.
Yet gold shines brighter, calling him near,
Whispering softly, allaying his fear.

In this waltz of elements, fire and ice,
A ribbon of truth, intertwined with vice.
He dances boldly through trials of old,
Forging his fate from lead and gold.

So let the music play, let spirits soar,
For life is a dance, forevermore.
With every twirl, both heavy and light,
In the heart of the storm, they find their flight.

Silver Linings in Hidden Glades

In glades where silver moonlight glows,
And whispers of magic flutter like prose.
Amid trees that weave their secrets low,
The heart finds peace where wildflowers grow.

A path forgotten, beneath the fern,
Leads to adventures for those who yearn.
Where sunlight dapples the forest floor,
And laughter sings through the closing door.

Each hidden glade, a realm of dreams,
Where the world is more than what it seems.
Nature's embrace, a soothing balm,
Beneath the stars, the night is calm.

With silver linings framing the dark,
Hope unfurls like the wings of a lark.
In quiet corners, love's gentle hum,
Calls out to all who wish to come.

So wander forth, let your spirit roam,
In glades of silver, you'll find a home.
For every shadow hides a light,
In hidden spaces, take to flight.

The Alchemist's Lament

In shadowed halls where silence weeps,
The weight of gold, the secret keeps.
A potion lost, dreams turned to stone,
In whispered winds, I walk alone.

The stars above, they mock my fate,
Transmute my heart, it's not too late.
With swirling skies and ancient dust,
I weave my fate, I dream, I trust.

But time, it flows like molten brass,
Elixirs born yet never passed.
In every spark, a promise glows,
A life undone, where longing grows.

Oh, fleeting joys, like mist, they fade,
When all is lost, I'm left dismayed.
Yet through the tears, a glimmer shines,
In every riddle, hope entwines.

I'll blend my sorrows with the night,
Transform despair into delight.
For in each trial, the truth's unveiled,
An alchemist, my heart will sail.

Glimmering Reflections in Dusty Corners

In corners worn by time's embrace,
Where whispers linger, secrets trace.
A flicker here, a shadow there,
The echoes dance in dusty air.

The moonlight spills on cobwebbed floors,
Unveiling tales of ancient wars.
With every glimmer, stories rise,
Of laughter lost and midnight sighs.

With trembling hands, I wipe away,
The layers thick of yesterday.
What once was bright, now softly gleams,
In shards of hope, I stitch my dreams.

The past, a tapestry of gold,
Of paths untaken yet retold.
In frames of dust, the moments gleam,
Reflections cast in twilight's beam.

Each speck of dust, a wishful spark,
A trace of light within the dark.
In every tear, a smile faints,
Chasing shadows where memory paints.

Twilight's Glow and Ancient Alloys

In twilight's glow, where secrets blend,
I forge my thoughts on iron's bend.
With ancient tales and whispered lore,
I seek the key to an open door.

In hands of gold, the stories twist,
Weaving magic through the mists.
Each hammer strike, the echoes bind,
A resonance of heart and mind.

The fire's dance, the shadows play,
Each glowing ember holds a sway.
With every spark, the night unveils,
The mysteries that fate entails.

In alloyed dreams of rust and flame,
I'll carve my path and etch my name.
For in the dark, a light still glows,
A brighter path the twilight knows.

So heed the whispers in the air,
For every fear, I'll lay to bare.
In twilight's arms, new strength I find,
Forging futures, heart aligned.

The Fabric of Forgotten Memories

In woven threads of time they lay,
Forgotten dreams from yesterday.
A tapestry of joys and fears,
Each stitch a tale, a mix of tears.

In faded hues, the colors bleed,
Of laughter shared and silent need.
The fabric frays, yet still it holds,
The stories whispered, softly told.

Through hands that grasp at drifting past,
The memory's fabric weaves a cast.
In every knot, a promise tight,
Of warmth revived in fading light.

But deeper threads beyond our sight,
Unravel pain while chasing light.
In corners lined with woven grace,
Forgotten hearts find their place.

Each thread a bond to bring us home,
Through twilight paths, no more to roam.
With every weave, the truth appears,
The fabric binds our hopes and fears.

Where Forgotten Alchemies Reside

In caverns deep where shadows play,
Old spells linger, lost to the day.
The whispers of potions, a faded dream,
In vials of glass, in a moonlit beam.

Crystals dance in the ghostly light,
Their colors bright, a magical sight.
Forgotten tomes lie piled high,
Dust motes swirl, as silence sighs.

Beneath the stones where secrets lie,
Wise spirits watch with a knowing eye.
Elixirs brewed from starlit skies,
Awaken hope in the heart's soft sighs.

The ancient art, once held with pride,
Now drifts with time, a fading tide.
Yet, in each heart, the fire glows,
For in every spark, the magic flows.

So come, dear dreamer, and take your flight,
Where forgotten alchemies shine bright.
Seek the elixir that calls your name,
And find the courage to stake your claim.

The Weft of Time's Gentle Touch

In a tapestry woven of moments past,
Threads of silver, shadows cast.
Each knot a story, a memory spun,
Gentle whispers of glories won.

The loom of life, it sways and bends,
With every heartbeat, the fabric mends.
Time dances softly, a fleeting seam,
Stitching together each cherished dream.

Colors fade and bright hues blend,
As seasons shift, and paths may wend.
Yet, in this weave, a pattern lies,
A comfort found beneath the skies.

Glimmers of laughter and echoes of tears,
Intertwined through the passing years.
The weft of time, so delicate, sweet,
In every strand, our lives repeat.

So pause to ponder the threads unspun,
In the grand design, each life is one.
Hold close your weaving, cherish the touch,
For in the fabric, there's meaning much.

Portraits in Threads Left Behind

In quiet corners of dusty rooms,
Framed in shadows, a silence looms.
Faded fabric and colors worn,
Tell tales of hearts that loved and mourned.

Each stitch a moment, a sweet embrace,
Portraits captured, time can't erase.
Embroidered dreams in delicate thread,
Life's tapestry where memories spread.

With every unraveling, a story unfolds,
Of journeys taken and legends bold.
A tapestry woven with wisdom's hand,
Each thread a spirit that makes us stand.

Through laughter and sorrow, shadows gleam,
In every portrait, a whispered dream.
May we remember, and never forget,
The love in threads, in patterns set.

So seek the stories in fabrics concealed,
In every patch, a life revealed.
Portraits linger, their voices entwined,
In the heart's quiet, they are defined.

Echoing Lullabies in Worn Textiles

In blankets soft, a cradle's song,
Echoes of night where dreams belong.
Threads of comfort, warm embrace,
Worn textiles weave a sacred space.

The lullabies hush the setting sun,
In whispered tones, two hearts become one.
Each frayed edge tells of love's embrace,
Memories tucked in every trace.

As time weaves on, the stories fade,
Yet in each fiber, the dreams are laid.
Through storms and calm, they hold us near,
In the fabric of life, there's nothing to fear.

Tattered quilts hold the warmth of years,
Each stitch a teardrop, each patch our cheers.
Echoing lullabies sing soft and low,
In worn textiles, the love will flow.

So wrap your heart in the tales they tell,
In every thread, let our memories dwell.
For in these fibers, sweet songs arise,
Echoing softly 'neath starlit skies.

Beneath the Surface

In quiet depths where shadows weave,
A world concealed, where spirits grieve.
The whispers call, both soft and low,
A tapestry of tales to show.

Footsteps echo on the stone,
In realms where silent thoughts are grown.
The currents twist with secrets spun,
A dance of light where dreams are won.

In darkness lies the hidden truth,
An ancient tale of fleeting youth.
The moonlight kisses water's skin,
While pulse of life begins to spin.

With every wave, a story flows,
An ebbing heart where magic grows.
The surface hides, yet reveals more,
Adventures waiting just offshore.

So dive, dear soul, into the blue,
Where wonders pulse and hearts renew.
For beneath the surface lies the key,
To worlds unseen, to set you free.

A Hidden Glow

In twilight's embrace, we find the light,
A spark within the endless night.
Soft glimmers dance upon the edge,
Where dreams emerge, a whispered pledge.

The path ahead, both dark and bright,
Guided by hope's elusive flight.
Through tangled woods and misty air,
A hidden glow, forever rare.

Each step we take, a story told,
Of wanders bold and hearts of gold.
Emerald leaves beneath the stars,
Illuminate our hidden scars.

As fireflies twinkle in the glade,
They weave a fate through light and shade.
In silence, whispers softly flow,
Unraveling threads of this aglow.

To cherish light, we find our way,
A lantern bright in shadows' sway.
Beneath the moon's watchful eye,
A hidden glow will never die.

The Art of Transmuted Echoes

In chambers deep, where echoes play,
An art of sound will guide the way.
Through whispered tones of soft refrain,
Life's tapestry begins to wane.

A melody of heartbeats' dance,
Each note a fleeting, fateful chance.
Transmuted voice of night and day,
Resonates in shades of gray.

From shadows cast by fleeting light,
The echoes forge our shared insight.
In sorrowed sighs, in laughter bright,
Their timeless song ignites the night.

The symphony of dreams entwined,
In every heart, a truth confined.
Through echoed hopes and whispered fears,
We find our strength throughout the years.

So listen close, dear wandering soul,
Let echoes weave and make you whole.
The art of sound unlocks the door,
To worlds unseen, forevermore.

Fragments of a Shimmering Dream

In realms where fragments softly gleam,
We wander through a half-lit dream.
Each shard of light, a tale of old,
Whispers of magic yet untold.

As stardust trails ignite the night,
A tapestry of hope ignites.
The echoes of forgotten past,
In shimmering hues, forever cast.

With every breath, the dream unfolds,
Adventures bound in shimmering folds.
Through misty paths and endless skies,
A journey waits for hearts that rise.

Beneath the stars, our spirits soar,
Embracing dreams, forevermore.
Fragments spark within the night,
Creating worlds of pure delight.

So gather dreams, both bright and rare,
In peace and joy, fill up the air.
For life, my friend, is but a seam,
Stitched together by a dream.

Gossamer Threads of Forgotten Legacies

In ancient lore, the whispers dwell,
Of gossamer threads, a woven spell.
Each stitch a story, lost yet found,
An echo of the past resound.

Through time's embrace, these tales reside,
In shadows cast by dreams we bide.
They linger near, like autumn leaves,
In every heart, a truth believes.

Legacies of love and strife,
Weaving through the fabric of life.
In every heart, a song is sung,
Of battles fought and tales begun.

With every turn of fate's design,
Threads intertwine, a sacred sign.
A tapestry of lost and seen,
Each thread a path to what has been.

So heed the call of voices past,
Their wisdom shared will ever last.
For gossamer threads, though faint and small,
Connect us all, one and all.

Whispers of Alchemical Threads

In shadows deep where secrets blend,
The potions swirl, the fates contend.
With delicate hands, the alchemist stirs,
Crafting wonders that time obscures.

A glimmering note in twilight's grace,
Circles of gold in a hidden space.
Elixirs whisper of worlds unheard,
Through murmured charms and ancient word.

Crimson vapors rise to the night,
Fleeting glimpses of hidden light.
Each drop a story, each swirl a dream,
The whispers weave through the silent stream.

In the heart of the forge, where magic flows,
Mixing with care, as the knowledge grows.
A tapestry spun of joy and dread,
Where fate is penned in silken thread.

The stars align on the alchemist's art,
Breathing life into each silent part.
With each incantation, a path is spun,
In the dance of twilight, all is one.

Enigmatic Weavings of Old

In the echoes of time, a loom does hum,
Weaving tales of what's yet to come.
Threads of gold and shadows bold,
Fables hidden, waiting to unfold.

An ancient spell in each fiber's twist,
Mysteries lingering in twilight's mist.
Patterns emerge from the fabric's breath,
Telling stories of love, life, and death.

Silken strands in the moon's soft glow,
Secrets kept where the wild winds blow.
The weaver knows what the heart conceals,
With every stitch, the past reveals.

A tapestry bright of laughter and tears,
Woven with wisdom through endless years.
Enigmatic tales of joy and strife,
In each intricate weave lies a life.

As the loom shudders with silent glee,
The stories dance as if to be free.
In twilight's embrace, they spin and twine,
A world of magic, a tapestry divine.

The Sorcerer's Tangle

In shadows of night where the sorcerers dwell,
A tangle of spells in a whispered shell.
Mystic energies flow without end,
Crafting enchantments, a force to bend.

With wands raised high and intentions clear,
The air crackles with magic near.
Each twist of fate leads to unseen roads,
In the labyrinth of the heart, mystery codes.

Herbs and crystals, their power combined,
In the cauldron's depths, the secrets entwined.
Eyes of fire and voices that sing,
A dance of shadows, the sorcery's ring.

In the heart of the night, shadows collide,
In every tangle, a choice to abide.
Threads of fate weave through dreams of despair,
As whispers of magic fill the air.

So beware of the sorcerer's snare at dawn,
For tangled paths lead you far beyond.
In every spell that the night may weave,
Lies the question of what we believe.

Echoes of Forgotten Alloy

In the ruins of time, echoes call,
Silvery whispers that rise and fall.
Alloys of iron, of gold, and of flame,
Glinting softly, yet none know their name.

Forged in the heart of a stormy night,
The metal gleams with an ethereal light.
Each chunk of alloy, a story of yore,
Resonates through what we adore.

Forgotten secrets in layers obscure,
A tale that beckons, mysterious and pure.
Through the echoing chambers where silence reigns,
The breath of the ages still softly remains.

With hammer and dream, the blacksmith sings,
Bonding materials as bright as the springs.
In each crafted piece, a soul is bestowed,
Through echoes and alloy, the wisdom flowed.

So tread gently where the ancients tread,
For echoes of history linger instead.
In the heart of the forge, the past finds its way,
In the alloy of dreams, let magic sway.

Crumbling Ornaments of the Past

In dusty halls where shadows creep,
Old treasures whisper, secrets deep.
Each tarnished frame, a tale to tell,
Of forgotten dreams, where memories dwell.

The echoes dance in twilight's glow,
A flicker of where the heart did go.
Fragments of laughter, sighs entwined,
In every chip, a story lined.

With every breath, the air grows thick,
Time's gentle hand a magic trick.
An ornament's memory, fragile and fraught,
Holds wisdom in dust, dreams once sought.

Yet in this wreckage, hope remains,
A phoenix rising from rusted chains.
For all that fades, our hearts can mend,
In crumbling beauty, beginnings blend.

So linger here, in twilight's grasp,
Embrace the stories that shadows clasp.
With every glance, we weave the past,
In crumbling ornaments, love holds fast.

Whispers from the Enchanted Dye

In cauldrons bubbling, secrets brew,
Colors dance, both old and new.
With every drop, a tale unfolds,
Of weaver's dreams and spun golds.

The air is thick with history's scent,
In vibrant shades, the spell is spent.
A tapestry woven from time and thread,
Each hue alive, each fable said.

Their whispers rise like morning mist,
While shadows linger, they can't resist.
The dye knows all, from joy to pain,
Emotions spread like a soft rain.

Through the fibers, magic seeps,
In every stitch, a promise keeps.
The heartbeats echo in every hue,
As colors breathe, they bloom anew.

So listen close, as colors call,
In every shade, find the rise and fall.
A symphony weaves through time's embrace,
In whispers from the enchanted space.

The Lament of Broken Artifacts

Once they shone in vibrant light,
Now lie shattered, lost from sight.
Echoes of laughter in every crack,
Memories cling, but time won't turn back.

In shards of glass, reflections fade,
Stories buried beneath the jade.
Artifacts whisper of times gone by,
In broken pieces, our dreams still sigh.

A teardrop falls upon the floor,
Each fracture tells of what was more.
Glimmers of magic in every piece,
In sorrow's wake, we seek release.

Through faded colors, histories bend,
In loss, there lies a chance to mend.
For every fragment, a world inside,
In the lament of artifacts, we bide.

So gather 'round these tales untold,
In broken beauty, we find the bold.
In every loss, a flicker ignites,
The heart of treasure, in long-lost sights.

A Nexus of Past and Present

In twilight's glow, where moments blend,
The past and now, two worlds send.
A whispering bridge of light and shade,
In every heartbeat, a story laid.

Through time's embrace, we often drift,
In memories held, we find our gift.
A dance of shadows, echoing bright,
Where futures glimmer, caught in flight.

The threads of history, woven tight,
In every glance, a spark ignites.
In laughter, echoes from days of yore,
In solace, find what we adore.

Caught in the tapestry of our fate,
We weave through time, we hesitate.
In every moment, a chance to learn,
A fusion of time, as candles burn.

So step upon this sacred path,
Embrace the warmth, let go your wrath.
In the nexus of what was and will be,
We find our place, we learn to see.

Beneath the Weave

In shadows spun by ancient hands,
A tapestry of dreams expands.
Where whispers weave the threads of fate,
In corners where the lost hearts wait.

With every stitch, a story breathes,
Of moonlit nights and tangled leaves.
The fabric hums with secrets old,
As tales of magic softly unfold.

Beneath the weave, enchantment lies,
In patterns drawn 'neath starlit skies.
A shimmering thread, a silver line,
Unraveling mysteries, pure divine.

The weaver's touch, both firm and light,
Transcending time, outshining night.
For those who seek, the truth shall gleam,
In the woven fabric of each dream.

So wander, brave soul, take your chance,
Beneath the weave, let your heart dance.
For every thread tells tales untold,
In the realm of magic, brave and bold.

Stones of Time

Upon the hill, the stones do sleep,
Guarding secrets, vast and deep.
Each one a witness, carved in time,
To echo histories, steeped in rhyme.

They shimmer softly in the light,
A relic of forgotten night.
With every glance, a memory stirs,
Of ancient kings and distant rivers.

Whispers travel on the breeze,
Lifting tales from roots of trees.
The stones, they beckon, stories crave,
From silent graves, a world to save.

In circles formed, they gather round,
As magic pulses through the ground.
Their sturdy hearts, steadfast as time,
Holding the past, both sweet and sublime.

Oh, listen close, and you might hear,
The voices swept away by fear.
In stones of time, a spark ignites,
Revealing wonders, hidden sights.

Nostalgia Woven with Elixirs

In bottles huddled on the shelf,
Lies the echo of one's self.
Each elixir, a sip of past,
Reviving moments meant to last.

With every drop, the memory swells,
In fragrant dreams and mystic spells.
A hint of laughter, a whisper of tears,
Floating softly through the years.

The potion's glow holds warmth so bright,
Illuminating shadows of the night.
A taste of joy, a dash of sorrow,
Forging paths to a tomorrow.

In nostalgia's grasp, we wander free,
Through hazy fields of reverie.
With every sip, a story calls,
As the elixirs weave their thrall.

So raise your glass, embrace the lore,
For life's elixirs hold so much more.
In every blend, both sharp and sweet,
The essence of our lives does meet.

The Scent of Olden Spells

Beneath the boughs of ancient trees,
The air is laced with whispered pleas.
A fragrance thick, of herbs and lore,
Where witches danced on twilight's floor.

With every breath, the past unfolds,
In scents of magic, rich and bold.
A blend of sage, and lavender's grace,
Invokes the spirits of this place.

Through tendrils of smoke, the echoes rise,
As shadows gather beneath the skies.
In cauldrons brewing, secrets churn,
For in their depths, our hearts still yearn.

The scent of olden spells enchants,
Inviting dreams and mystic chants.
With each soft waft, the magic swells,
A bridge to times of long-lost spells.

So come, dear seeker, breathe it in,
This fragrant dance where dreams begin.
In scents of magic, we are bound,
In every whisper of the ground.

Echoes of Luster and Decay

In twilight's glow, the echoes play,
Of luster lost and bright decay.
Each shimmer fades, yet still inspires,
A dance of shadows, whispered fires.

The vibrant hues, they speak of life,
In fleeting moments, joy and strife.
Yet through the dim, the beauty gleams,
As time unveils forgotten dreams.

In crumbling walls and gilded frames,
Reside the whispers of lost names.
We walk where echoes softly tread,
In a tapestry of light and dread.

For every glimmer, a story hides,
Of laughter shared and broken tides.
In both the luster and the pain,
Resilience blossoms, like summer rain.

So heed the echoes, let them stay,
In every luster, every decay.
For through the years, they softly sing,
Of life's sweet cycles, endless spring.

Echoes of a Tarnished Tale

In the silence of the night, whispers creep,
Old fears awaken from their slumber deep.
A story etched in shadows long ago,
Where light once danced, now only echoes flow.

Beneath the silver glow of faded dreams,
The heart speaks softly, unraveling seams.
With every heartbeat, fragments come alive,
In the depths of memory, truths survive.

Once vibrant laughter fades like morning mist,
As bitter moments fade and twist.
We stand upon the edge of what was lost,
With every echo, we remember the cost.

Threads of fate entwine like ivy's embrace,
In the web of time, we seek our place.
Yet hope remains, a flickering flame,
In tarnished tales, we find our name.

So let the night enfold our haunted song,
For in the darkness, we will learn to be strong.
Each echo holds a lesson yet untold,
In a tarnished tale, we are bold.

Mysteries Woven in Starlight

Beneath the canvas of a velvet sky,
Where stars whisper secrets, dreams flutter by.
Each twinkle holds a story waiting to bloom,
In the quiet night, banishing gloom.

The cosmos dances in a mystic trance,
Inviting the souls of night to take a chance.
Through shimmering threads of destiny spun,
We chase the echoes of every sun.

Glimmers of silver glide across our path,
A gentle reminder of the aftermath.
Lost between the shadows, we search for light,
For mysteries woven in starlit night.

Each heartbeat syncs with the rhythm so divine,
As the universe whispers, "This moment is thine."
Veils of enchantment drape our weary heads,
In the tapestry of night, the past gently threads.

So sail upon the dreams that tide the shore,
For mysteries in starlight are forevermore.
In every flicker, a promise anew,
Woven in starlight, our spirits grew.

Shards of Moonlight in the Fabric

In the depths of night, the moonlight falls,
Crafting silver shards that gently call.
Each glimmer a fragment, a piece of the whole,
In the fabric of dreams, they stir the soul.

Threads of soft whispers under the veil,
Carry the secrets of a time-worn tale.
With every shimmer that dances on skin,
We awaken the magic that dwells within.

Winds weave through the branches, a gentle sigh,
Echoing tales of the past as they fly.
In moonlit shadows, we find our way,
Through the labyrinth of night, come what may.

The fabric of dreams entwined with our fate,
Each shard of moonlight, a thread we create.
As we wander the paths of what lies ahead,
In the tapestry woven, our hearts are fed.

So let the moon guide us with its soft grace,
In the night's embrace, we find our place.
Shards of moonlight, a luminous map,
In the fabric of evening, we lovingly wrap.

Gilded Shadows of Arcane Weaving

In the twilight hour, shadows start to twine,
With whispers of magic in the air, divine.
Gilded threads shimmer where mysteries lie,
In the woven tapestry, our spirits fly.

Each shadow dances with secrets to share,
As ancient spells linger in the cool night air.
Under the watchful gaze of silver orbs,
We seek the magic that the darkness absorbs.

With every flicker of candlelight's glow,
The arcane weaving begins to bestow.
In the corners of night, wonder takes its flight,
Through gilded shadows, we embrace the light.

Bound by enchantment, we find our way,
In the labyrinth of dreams, we choose to stay.
A symphony echoes through the silent space,
Where shadows and magic lovingly embrace.

So join the dance of the unseen and known,
In the gilded shadows, we have grown.
With each woven thread, our story unfolds,
In the arcane tapestry, our heart's truth holds.

The Richness of Unseen Colors

In twilight's grasp, soft hues take flight,
A tapestry woven in the fading light.
Emerald whispers in the breeze,
Nature's palette hidden with ease.

The sky unveils a quiet glow,
With secrets only dreamers know.
Each sunset drapes a silken sheet,
Unseen colors at their feet.

The stars emerge in velvet black,
A galaxy's jewel-studded track.
In silence, they paint the night,
With brushes dipped in pure delight.

Beyond the eye, the heart can see,
The rich embrace of harmony.
In vibrant shades of joy and grace,
Life blooms in each enchanted space.

With every glance, a story spins,
A symphony where hope begins.
In unseen colors, truths reside,
A world of wonder, our hearts guide.

A Fabric of Shadows and Light

In the quiet corners of the mind,
A fabric weaves of the intertwined.
Shadows dance with a subtle grace,
Whispers echo in a sacred space.

Threads of darkness, stitched with care,
In every fold, a hidden prayer.
Light breaks forth, a gentle stream,
Illuminating what we dream.

In twilight's art, the world transforms,
A ballet played by unseen forms.
Each heartbeat signals the night's embrace,
Where shadows and light find their place.

Tales of old and futures bright,
Intertwine in the soft moonlight.
A fabric spun from fears and hopes,
Crafting pathways as the heart copes.

In echoes soft, the truth unspools,
A dance of wisdom, a dance of fools.
Together they weave the tale divine,
A fabric of shadows, where stars align.

Threads Spun from Silent Whispers

In the hush between the leaves,
Silent whispers every heart perceives.
Threads of longing knot and weave,
Within the night, where dreams believe.

Ethereal voices, soft as dew,
Crafting stories, ancient and new.
With each murmur, spirits gleam,
Bound by the magic of a dream.

The tapestry stretches, wide and deep,
A promise made, a promise to keep.
In the shadows, where secrets roam,
Whispers guide the weary home.

Each thread a memory, sweet and bitter,
The dance of life, the joy and shiver.
Through every silence, a world unfurls,
Mysteries wrapped in softest pearls.

With delicate care, the loom does spin,
A fortune told in the quiet din.
Threads of whispers, strong and bright,
In the heart's embrace, they find their light.

The Legacy of Rusting Gold

In the cellar's gloom, forgotten dreams,
Rusting treasures fade at the seams.
Fractured memories, once so bright,
Dimming slowly, lost to the night.

Gold that shimmered with radiant fire,
Now a legacy, a ghostly pyre.
Echoes of laughter cling to the air,
In the remnants of moments, once rare.

Each tarnished piece a tale to tell,
Of love that blossomed and bids farewell.
In the quiet, a promise takes hold,
For beauty lingers in rusting gold.

Time weaves its tapestry rich and vast,
Each stitch a memory of the past.
As life cycles, it whispers so sweet,
In decay, there's a story complete.

Legacy lies in the hearts we share,
In every spark, in every prayer.
With every shimmer that fades away,
Rusting gold leads us gently to stay.

The Ethereal Spindle's Song

In twilight's hush, the spindle spins,
Whispers of magic, where the light begins.
Threads of silver in the cool night air,
Dance like starlight, weaving dreams with care.

Each twist a story, each turn a sigh,
Echoes of ancient fables floating high.
The fabric of time, it catches the stars,
With every heartbeat, the universe jars.

Woven in colors of dusk and dawn,
Memories linger, though the day is gone.
Hauntingly sweet, the spindle's refrain,
Calls to the lost, reviving their pain.

Within the fibers, enchantments reside,
Promises whispered, a tumultuous ride.
In shadows that lacquer the world we know,
A tapestry blooms, where dreams softly flow.

So listen closely, to the soft melody,
The song of the spindle, alive and free.
In each gentle motion, the cosmos replies,
A dance of creation beneath velvet skies.

Arcana in the Weave

Hidden in strands where the moonlight flickers,
Ancient spells pulse, like time's steady tickers.
Threads interlace, in patterns divine,
Revealing the secrets that stars would confine.

Each fiber a whisper in the still of the night,
Binding the dreamers with silvery light.
The weaver's hands glide through shadows and glow,
Crafting the stories that only they know.

Arcane enchantments breathe life into seams,
Fashioning wanderers' soft, silken dreams.
Currents of magic begin to unwind,
As the tapestry pulses, and fate's thread entwined.

Caught in a web of celestial grace,
The weavers of fate obscure time and space.
With every connection, a choice made anew,
In the heart of the fabric, all paths are revealed.

So treasure each strand, both fragile and bold,
For within its embrace lies a legend retold.
In every entwining of thread you shall see,
The arcana of life, a vibrant tapestry.

Celestial Patterns Unspooled

Stars in the heavens, glimmer and sway,
Crafted in patterns that dance and play.
Each constellation, a tale from afar,
Unspooled in the night, like a wish on a star.

Winding like rivers through an infinite sky,
The fibers of fate, like whispers they fly.
Secrets are hidden within every loop,
In cosmic endeavors, the universe stoops.

Every thread bears the weight of a story,
Beneath the sky's veil, in radiant glory.
In the loom of existence, the patterns shall twirl,
As destinies intertwine and unfurl.

Celestial patterns, in grandeur displayed,
In twilight's embrace, all doubts shall cascade.
Each moment a stitch in the fabric of time,
In the symphony spun, the cosmos will chime.

So gaze at the heavens, and ponder the weft,
In the tapestry woven, we are never bereft.
For every heartbeat echoes through all,
In destiny's loom, we rise and we fall.

Enchanted Fibers of the Night

In the quiet twilight, where shadows embrace,
Enchanted fibers weave magic with grace.
Spinning together, the night's gentle sigh,
A fabric of wonder that dreams cannot die.

Threads of enchantment twinkling like stars,
Whispers of lore, healing old scars.
Each stitch a promise spun with delight,
Bringing forth magic to chase away night.

Beneath silver moonbeams, the weavers align,
Creating a canvas, the edges divine.
Every colored strand tells a story anew,
As the night weaves its fabric, in patterns so true.

A tapestry brightens as dreams intertwine,
Casting aside shadows, with threads that define.
In each tender loop, we find solace and rest,
As the fibers of night cradle hearts at their best.

So hold close the essence of magic and light,
In enchanted fibers that shimmer through night.
For with every weave, a new journey takes flight,
In the heart of the night, where magic feels right.